Raw Opals

Illuminati

Lyn
Lifshin

Raw Opals

Some of these poems were published in

Berkeley Review
The Centennial Review
Confrontation
Cream City Review
Grain
Greenfield Review
Groundswell
The Hollins Critic
Kaldron
The Literary Review
New Letters
Paintbrush
Poetry East
Poetry Now
Sojourner
Vagabond
Webster Review
Wormwood Review

"Thank you" to Yaddo and
Millay Colony, where some of
these poems were written

Illuminati
P.O. Box 67E07
Los Angeles 90067

Printed in USA
ISBN: 0-89807-251-4

Raw Opals

I was four, in dotted

Swiss summer pajamas
my face a blotch of
measles in the small
dark room over blue
grapes and rhubarb,
hot stucco cracking
17 North Seminary
that July Friday
noon my mother was
rushed in the grey
blimp of a Chevy
north to where my
sister Joy would be
born two months
early. I wasn't
ready either and
missed my mother's
cool hands, her
bringing me frosty
glasses of pineapple
juice and cherries
with a glass straw
as Nanny lost her
false teeth, flushed
them down the toilet
then held me so tight
I could smell lavendar
and garlic in her
braided hair   held

me as so few ever
have since   as if
not to lose more

After gliding back

the stillness of pines
with only skiis slicing
the blue   and the rooster
piercing the black light
still wrapping us   even
back in the house where
our boots dripped on
sleek wood and you said
let's see if the electric
blanket still works. My
phone like a siren, my
mother signalling, ring
ing once   ringing again
then starting over. Her
aloneness in the apart
ment she never fixed up
and won't, two doors from
where my uncles are sell
ing the stores suddenly.
My mother asks if I want,
before the doors are
nailed down, a blue vase
from Italy, towels to
match the ones I still
haven't used. Something
in her scared and wild
as an animal whose food
is being torn away, a
blanket of loss and

darkness wrapping her.
That darkness like the
ashes of someone cremated
I'm trying to scatter
over the Hudson, blow
ing back in my face

In 1923

the blue stucco starts
flaking, cracks between
boards in the floor
pull apart. My mother
in the smallest of the
bedrooms, being a
girl, in the one
with no heat writing
FML on frost. Her
brothers are brought
orange juice in high
feather beds light
is wild as raw opals
she thinks of the rag
between her legs
she'll have to wash
out of the blood
trail thru elms when
the cat dragged her
self back from Dr.
Goss on 3 legs thru
cracked branches,
her mother's yelp at
Buffy, less muffled
than when she caught
her husband in the
den with the Polish
girl as the future
grew like a scar

4:30 am

words on tape,
a blood moon
falling into my
bed. I roll
near the wild
light   my
hair sleeps
with your words
love you said I
never write a
word about what
I don't know.
The jungle,
steamy blood
on leaves a
woman's hand
in a mass
grave pulling
on you. Typing
out the dark
ness ghosts
in quinine
wind. Saigon
branches in
your ruined
house you take
a breath
it was random you
say a gun

in the drawer
humans aren't
fragile they
will do anything

It's like the rose I carried thru windy airport runways

already dying
only tea rose in
my hair made
people turn   gasp
at withered
petals   imagine
those leaves
were filling the
room with a
sweetness   I
wanted to trap
that color
in melted candles
I'd have frozen
it in a cube
of glass pressed
it in a dictionary
because of whose
lips had touched
it   like where
you touched Sunday

Golden Gate Park

pink leaves
in the gazebo

tangerine flowers
cats   Japanese

girl in cut offs.
You took photo

graphs of me

never took me

Leaving Rome

olive branches slap
chrome   the sky's a
blue clearer than
agates. Cobblestones,
arches balanced as
precariously as our
words in the car
as if we both knew
something besides
the trip was ending
tho lulled in the
over grown amphi
theater where rose
light licked our
skin and turned
hair mahogany.
Frascati helped
make the black
glow tho stones in
us were falling
like those in the
basilica at Saint
Sebastian and we
were as scratched,
dug into and dark
as the catacombs
where frescoes
peal and those
waiting for the
Nazis huddled,
clinging to stones

Downstairs the dark studded

with glow of
white branches
clots of snow,
stars in clumps.
You have to bury
your face in
white. In
Syracuse, off
Comstock, the
lilacs just
starting the
first man who
touched me
inside my
clothes pulled
me under such
white boughs
thru rain dripping
lacy boughs, light
filling the
dark orchard
in this same
jeweled light
everything
opening like
these clenched buds

Yellow Roses

pinned on stiff tulle,
glowed in the painted
high school moonlight.
Mario Lanza's "Oh My
Love." When Doug
dipped, I smelled
Clearasil. Hours in
the tub dreaming of
Dick Wood's fingers
cutting in, sweeping
me close. I wouldn't
care if the stuck
pin on the roses
went thru me,
the yellow musk
would be a wreath
on the grave of that
awful dance where
Louise and I sat
pretending we didn't
care, our socks fat
with bells and fuzzy
ribbons, bloated and
silly as we felt   I
wanted to be home
wanted the locked
bathroom to cry in
knew some part of me
would never stop
waiting to be
asked to dance

Maybe he had just read Heart Of Darkness

or it was the moon
refusing to give up
its bald head   glowing
like a huge hole
longer than was natural
when he got to where he
wanted to be in me
at the end he's ship
wrecked   and saw me
as a black river
he couldn't get a
way inside   dark water
already stained his
hands and he was
dizzy from a strange
fever. But he had
chosen this trip   he
wanted to get to where
when he didn't he
felt lost in fog and
dreams and night
mare. When he
pressed me into
his skin then
it was as if every
thing close to
him was mirror
he saw bodies and
glistening skin in
my leaves   it was
hard to breathe

the dark held
him like hands

Depression

a black sand black
waves are licking,
making holes the
darkest water
rises in. Mid
night floods the
house climbs
stairs like a
six foot 3 dancer
in a hurry. Soon
the quilt's drenched
in it. Dressers
float toward the
street   the waves
lap words from
poems   strip
Tuesday of its
green like a
tree becoming
driftwood

East River Trail

unless you stop
you don't see
wild hemlock
poking pewter
sky. Their roots
bulge thru needles
like toes that
have outgrown
too tight shoes.
In hot light,
pines steam
like soup. My
heart's loud
as a stomach.
When I stop a
lake is wild
in the light
so far down it
seems a glass
bead. It's been
all uphill as
if only what's
hard to get
to matters

Deer

the death of one
feeds so many coyotes

the way people seem
starved for a

dead poet's poems

Another young woman disappears in the trees

on a night I
drove lost on dark
streets with people
leering on stoops
the first March
night it's close to
80. She took a
bus on a parallel
street feeling the
night air that made
my hair curly, my
skin melt under
pink leather pants
the day after my
car broke down
on the road where
she was last seen
walking stopped
suddenly in the
windy light cars
slamming past. I
was lucky the man
who stopped took
me to the garage
she'd decided to
save money maybe
so hitched or walked
with a knapsack like
the book bag I
carried   air wild,
smelling of things

unfolding her
hair long and amber
too. You might
suppose she isn't
missing, but escaped
in my clothes   is
hiding out some
where inside me.
But I've put what
ever's most
          vulnerable in me
          outside me, so its
          hardened, is the
          leather I use as
          a disguise. She still
          believed in everything

Getting rid of what I can't use

these men are like
fat, making it hard
to move right, a
pain when you try
to bend or leave
the house. They
clot, the result
of a weak moment,
temptation late
with the moon too
bright in a room
you'd rather just
sleep in. You bulge,
an overcrowded
motel. What fills
you doesn't consider
much. Scales zoom
past where you'd
thought they'd be,
wild as last year's
resolutions. It's
hard to breathe.
When you start to
dance they're a
strain on your
heart

After the reading

the man with a rubber
band around "Death
in the Afternoon"
lumbers up to the podium, asks for
my autograph on a
Greyhound ticket
keeps pointing his
finger to Hemingway's
name, says they
don't have tv there
but there's more
inside and asks,
shaking, stopping
between words like
a deer that hears
something rustling
in the leaves, if I know
about dementia praecox
stubble on his cheek
a silky red tie, his
long fingers tug at,
eyes like marbles
in a jar in a car that
zig zags thru corners,
pale light banging
into glass

In that house

mahogany peals
under dresser
scarves of lace.
Maple darkening
bedrooms. Porch
screens rust,
slow as lines
branching out
under skin. The
candelabra is
turning black.
In ripple glass
a woman presses
amber beads
to her skin as
if to suck up
the only light

the woman in the mirror
unloosens
long burnt maple
hair, feels the
walls suck on
her like air
swirling in
shells, turn
into January
splinters. When
she touches her
skin it's as if
with someone
else's fingers.

If that man
were to come
looking for some
one smelling of
roses and lavendar
he'd just find
long strands
of hair in a
comb, dresses
in a closet

Like dogs left out near the crumbling adobe

old dogs   people
have dumped   left
out in the country
the people soothe
their minds with
thoughts that the
old dogs might
catch a chicken
and live   My
husband and I
would walk around
sunset   the adobe
rose in the last
light   rose and
cantaloupe sand
with the dogs
howling   the
ones that still
could   My husband
would put his
arms around me
tight   tighter
I don't know how
people could be
so cruel he said
how heartless   I
was 30 then   my
hair smelled of
pinon and I thought
I'd gotten over

things I was afraid
of   30 years later
and I could be
those dogs   I
don't know where
my next meal will
come from   a
bandonned like
those old sick
dogs   my junior
league card in
my wallet next
to New Mexico
foodstamps

For three days things kept changing

suitcases were open
graves she'd fill
with silk scarves
and cats to make
sure they wouldn't
swallow her,   the
postcards from
Denver curl in
damp heat   she
strips to bra
and panties,
as if terror
was a lover
with such a
strong tongue,
fingers opening
what no one
could keep
closed, as if
what was hidden
in folds   black
as a night tulip
was the note
in a bottle
her fingers
would shrivel
trying to reach

Next door my neighbor is moving

packing the Chinese
rugs and amethyst
measuring the
Chippendale chest
she's circled which
crates are for
silver which for
moving china this
year she won't
see the grape
vine turn green
from her bed the
Chinese dogwood's
star flowers glow
across the yard
from lawnchairs a
June breeze hits
40 years she's
watched her husband
put in rose leaves
and iris   a border
of geraniums that
never looked the
same when she put
them in herself
alone   she's pack
ing the years she
painted while he
played the violin
told her what to
pack for Paris   his

voice as much a part
of the rooms as the
way light slivers
thru the spruce
that was just planted
the first night in
the house, the moon
wild on them the
whole night

The old woman in Amsterdam

like someone who feels
she'll be pressed in
the dark of earth long
later, she walked with
all her windows open
nude   skin flapping
like fingers signing
in a house of blind
men. She cuts maples
to stubs to let sun
eat her. Left shutters
open in the rain to
feel her hair flow
like linden dust
didn't want anything
heavy as earth on her
yet   slept on top of
a pile of blue quilts
as if her life was
leaves resting on a
lake fish drift up
in thru dark water

The Lanae, Hotel Kaiamona

The Japanese girl
waiting 7 hours
under the hau tree
holds the same
drink   watching thru
its water   the sand
blackens   Diamond
Head eats the sun she
twists hair like a
ring around her
finger   pink
leaves brown
on the floor   she
is telling of those
apples in the mountains
that don't need cold
like plums but sweeter
smiles but she
won't leave   come
with us   stays tho
the candles are burning
is like those birds
in Africa that fly
for hours hardly beating
their wings but they
can't land   crash
breaking their
beaks   blinded maybe
and paralyzed
going around in
shock back and
forth to their nests
not understanding

Rose Devorah

dreams of old houses
in Russia, licorice hair
fire licks as lace is
scorched, turns ash
before the wedding
and the bride's bones
are dust in the
rose light green is
sucked from as sun
sets in the after
noon. Some unknown
aunt she could have
been named for maybe
wild, intense as rare
tea roses or Rashmi
Rose incense burnt in
a room the walls
pulled from floats
thru frames that are
like mirrors, her
raw cheeks like
cherries in the rain
or blood from a wild
deer running, turning
snow color of plums

Steepletop

smell the last
apples in the moon light
knowing someone else
would walk among these
dark apples having
lost what they
were sure they could
never live without
not what they'd
been or planned on
becoming   holding
a cold apple
and feeling it
warm as they held it

Millay   hearing the news

it was as if she
was the snow
the buck's blood
gushed out on,
turning the color
of what he lost

she walked out on
to the platform and
the words were her
friends   it was

as if she was
walking under
water   three weeks
later she remembered
the wine specially
made for her

like finding a letter
with what hadn't
and should have
been said, unmailed

the day after the funeral.
For the rest of the
show   blood that had
frozen in her wouldn't
dissolve   when

she went out on
stage tho the words
came out as if the
ghost of the dead

poet was breathing
in her   it was

the way wind catches
in the fur of the
dead cat near

rt 20   and what moves
seems to come
from inside

Basil

all the way down the
sloped hill under
the white pines
you should pick it while
the sun is low and night's
water is wild on the
red grass   don't kick up
the sweet lace   twist
or crunch out the smell
but pick it while it's
sucking up afternoon
light   its smell on
your fingers like
a lover   let it
inside   pin it to
beams in rooms apricot
light will sneak thru
glazing bare walnuts
knowing the leaves
still wait in snow
full of what drew
you to it

Reeds in snow

like women with long
hair running out of
a burning building
dazed,   half frozen
from a hotel room
of clothes and rings
from dead relatives
or a handwritten
manuscript there's
no other copy of

The thought of it

hangs in the air
presses down like
smoke on a day
you smell rain
coming   you
try to take
a deep breath   it
circles Saturday
like some huge
Goodyear blimp
gloating over
houses   slapping
shadows on
teacups,
thighs

My mother and the matches

She said I didn't know you
couldn't either my mother
who knew which man was
circumcised and which
woman's laugh I like

Light matches? no we both
laugh we couldn't and
nearly flunked chemistry
One day when my lab partner
didn't come the bunsen
burner stayed unlit

At Raven's I cripple four
cardboard boxed matches and
can't admit I'm afraid
to be burnt

a whole year dreaming of
fires, my mother up all night
other Aprils sniffing
for smoke. My

mother had once said you
mean you'd swallow it but
she never until this
morning talked about
her fear of matches

startling as knowing she
has a down quilt from
Russia in a closet
I've never seen I

tell her I never lit a candle
till the lights went out that
fall for two days and then

I lit it on the electric
stove   never cooked tea
in a house with a
gas stove

Blue cabin in Maine
with just the wood stove
that had to be kept burning
I hardly slept 3 days

and do you hate to kill flies my
mother asks like Columbus
discovering a new continent

Barnstable two years ago

reeds and marsh
grass a frozen grey.
the cat locked in one
room at Murray's
we walked, my mother
with more energy than
she'll have again
along route 1 to the
only restaurant.
torn branches
litter of broken
glass we had to
yell to hear each
other over cars,
bitching, laughing
feeling sun thru
winter coats

In my mother's bedroom

with the lights off
in the living room
the shades moving
from the first breeze
in eleven days
and the door shut so
the cat doesn't eat
needles   or ash
"here take this mirror"
my mother says pulling
open a drawer before
the huge mirror
I'd sit before studying
my legs   studying
the first swell of
nipples   I always stand
here with my skirt
raised when I come
home   my mother combing
my hair as I sat
on the same hassock
before its top was
replaced with blue cloth
my hair just as curly
as hers then years
before I would have a
hair like the one
she doesn't want on
the same place on
my chin as hers is

Holding animals

the warm fur, like
a quilt or bunting.
Memento on the
velvet squares, a
warm potato or stone
travelers would
wrap in wool for
sleigh rides the
first night it
snowed or put in
dark beds in icy
mansions. A child
in tears burying
her neck in some
smelly dog's neck.
The waves of breath
like waves smooth
ing ragged edges
my aunt, after her
19 year old child
is buried clutched
the ragged black
and white cat to
her as if what she
held   held her

My mother straightening pots and pans

"I can't see why you
keep so many coffee pots
with cracked handles"
she frowns as if looking
at a police line up
where all the faces
were lovers who'd
slid thru my arms
"you've got a lot of
junk but nothing to
make something hearty
you need pots that
would last a life
they don't make pots
or men as the used to"

My mother's third call on a day of sleet and december falling

as if the whiteness was
gauze wrapped over the
mouth of someone dying
and she had to slash it
with a last word, or
Monday was a blank
sheet of paper only my
words would cling to.
My mother, who lugged
suitcases with me in the
78 blizzard when subways
broke in Brooklyn, says
the wind crossing the
street wouldn't let
her breathe. I'm stand
ing with my hair dripping,
turning the quilt a darker
blue   the water boiling
downstairs, thinking how
long it's been since I've
gone to visit her   or
haven't told her I had
to rush   but just let the
words between us wrap
us like the navy afghan
on the velvet couch with
the stain where the grey
cat peed and just drifted
in the closeness   linked
as we once were   as if
we always would be

There were blue grapes behind the house

grey painted wide boards
bugs could sleep in.
Wasps still sliver thru
the screens on 38 Main St.
and the lilac room is
24 shades of plum
the sun's tongue only
went so far. Shards.
Rooms. Pieces. Stuck
to each other like
the glass in teapots
glazed with hair like
cracks, like a fat
woman held tight in
nylon so she seems some
body else. Like slices
of music, a little
Bach some old black
jazz   all the world's
music from the stone
ages on a 90-minute
cassette packed into
Voyager on a trip with
no known end thru
the stars

My sister in dripping pines and yews and maple

in April dark light,
rain bending rhinestone
branches into mud.
10am's a dark rose
that won't flower.
My sister curls in a
chair he wouldn't want
her feet up in with
32 years of diaries.
Mist rises from ponds
like sketched hot
July Tuesdays in the
apartment where wasps
dripped to the floor
and Otter Creek blurred
fighting. She is in
film run backward   38
16   about 8   thick
legs pared down   thin
in toe shoes the
ribbons never were
sewed right on. The
words, green   pressed
by what was heavy
closed and stored in
darkness like a
lilac corsage   are
fragile and thin
as a life pressed
to paper   hard to

touch as those days,
as rare and as
longed for

That cat's yelp in black light

pine needles dripping,
covering cars deeper than
mist. My sister is pulled
toward what tore night
like a child in pain
to where the cat drags
one half of his body
thrashing and tangling
through legs of chair
no light's touched.
We wrapped his
writhing in flannel
drove on winding roads
thru maple hills,
black fur flinching
reaching toward noon.
Nothing to do but wait.
we were shaking, numb
bought butter pecan
ice cream that dripped
down skin like tears.
Embolism. White pines
blackening. Next
morning the vet says
the cat died in the
night. A sack of clots,
a whole heartful. My
sister doesn't stop
clearing the table,
packs the car   it's as
if the cat's wet fur

and twitching have
moved inside her